IT'S MY STATE! ★

NORTH CAROLINA

Ann Graham Gaines

Andy Steinitz

Marshall Cavendish
Benchmark
New York

Published by Marshall Cavendish Benchmark
An imprint of Marshall Cavendish Corporation

Website: www.marshallcavendish.us

This publication represents the opinions and views of the authors based on their personal experience, knowledge, and research. The information in this book serves as a general guide only. The authors and publisher have used their best efforts in preparing this book and disclaim liability rising directly and indirectly from the use and application of this book.

Other Marshall Cavendish Offices:
Marshall Cavendish International (Asia) Private Limited, 1 New Industrial Road, Singapore 536196 •
Marshall Cavendish International (Thailand) Co Ltd. 253 Asoke, 12th Flr, Sukhumvit 21 Road, Klongtoey Nua, Wattana, Bangkok 10110, Thailand • Marshall Cavendish (Malaysia) Sdn Bhd, Times Subang, Lot 46, Subang Hi-Tech Industrial Park, Batu Tiga, 40000 Shah Alam, Selangor Darul Ehsan, Malaysia

Marshall Cavendish is a trademark of Times Publishing Limited

All websites were available and accurate when this book was sent to press.

Library of Congress Cataloging-in-Publication Data
Gaines, Ann
        North Carolina / Ann Graham Gaines and Andy Steinitz. — 2nd ed.
               p. cm. — (It's my state!)
        Includes index.
        ISBN 978-1-60870-057-8
        1. North Carolina—Juvenile literature. I. Steinitz, Andy. II. Title.
     F254.3.G35 2011
     975.6—dc22   2010003930

Second Edition developed for Marshall Cavendish Benchmark by RJF Publishing LLC (www.RJFpublishing.com)
Series Designer, Second Edition: Tammy West/Westgraphix LLC
Editor, Second Edition: Stephanie Fitzgerald

All maps, illustrations, and graphics © Marshall Cavendish Corporation. Maps and artwork on pages 6, 34, 35, 75, 76, and back cover by Christopher Santoro. Map and graphics on pages 8 and 47 by Westgraphix LLC.

The photographs in this book are used by permission and through the courtesy of:
Front cover: Mary Terriberry/Shutterstock and Radius Images/Alamy (inset).
Alamy: Joel Zatz, 11; Chris A. Crumley, 16; Thomas R. Fletcher (top), 18; North Wind Picture Archives, 22, 25, 27, 31; David Kennedy, 30; INTERFOTO, 40; Tina Manley/North America, 44; Jeff Greenberg, 46; Clark Brennan, 53; Ilene MacDonald, 58, 65; Frank Tozier, 61; Andre Jenny, 67; Jim Hogue, 69; Jon Arnold Images Ltd., 73. *AP Images:* Terry Renna, 56. *Everett Collection:* Fred Norris/© The CW, 74. *Getty Images:* Bob Pool, 4; Tracy Morgan (top), 5; Bloomberg (bottom), 5, 64; Heinrich van den Berg, 20; Jeff Foott (right) and Gary Carter (left), 21; Bridgeman Art Library, 28; Ed Lallo/Time & Life Pictures, 33; MPI/Stringer/Hulton Archive, 37; Buyenlarge/Hulton Archive, 38; Time & Life Pictures, 39; FPG/Hulton Archive, 41; Jason Merritt/WireImage (right) and Wesley Hitt (left), 49; Steve Dunwell, 50; Logan Mock-Bunting, 52; Melissa Farlow, 54; Kevin C. Cox, 55; Ericka McConnell, 66; Tim Graham (bottom), 70; Lester Lefkowitz, 71. *Library of Congress:* LC-USZC4-2566, 48. *Office of the Governor, State of North Carolina:* 63. *Shutterstock:* David Kay, 10; Robert Donovan, 12; John Ray Upchurch, 14; Mary Terriberry, 15; Bonita R. Cheshier (bottom), 18; iofoto, 19; Stanislav Khrapov, 51; Travel Bug, 57; Robert Donovan, 70.

Printed in Malaysia (T).
135642

CONTENTS

State Bird: Cardinal

The North Carolina legislature chose this beautiful red bird as the state bird in 1943. Cardinals live in North Carolina year-round in huge numbers. Also known as the winter redbird, this fine singer can be spotted across the state.

State Flower: Flowering Dogwood

The dogwood is actually a flowering tree. Dogwoods grow all over the state—from the mountains to the coast. The trees flower only in spring, but the dogwood's leafy green foliage lasts through the summer.

State Tree: Pine

There are eight kinds of pine trees in North Carolina. In the colonial era, these trees and their sticky sap were important for making ships. The longleaf pine thrives in the sandy soil of the coastal plain. Longleafs actually need small wildfires for survival. The fires create rich soil nutrients that help the trees grow.

State Dog: Plott Hound

This hunting dog was first bred in the mountains of North Carolina around 1750. These gentle and loyal dogs were used to hunt wild boars. They are also skilled trackers. The Plott Hound is one of only four breeds of dog known to have started in the United States.

State Reptile: Eastern Box Turtle

Eastern box turtles can be found in forests, swamps, and fields throughout the state. They eat both plants and animals: fruits, berries, mushrooms, snails, slugs, worms, even dead frogs and ducks. When they are threatened, the turtles pull their head, tail, and limbs all the way into their shell and hide safely inside. The average lifespan of an eastern box turtle is fifty years, but some can live to be a hundred.

State Rock: Granite

Granite formed underneath the Piedmont region hundreds of millions of years ago. The world's largest open-faced granite quarry is located in Surry County. The quarry, known as "The Rock," is one mile (1.6 kilometers) long. It has supplied granite for use in buildings, bridges, and monuments all over the United States.

NORTH CAROLINA

Appalachian Mountains

Blue Ridge Mountains

Blue Ridge Parkway

Great Smoky Mountains

Mount Mitchell

Nantahala Lake

Great Dismal Swamp

Yadkin River

Greensboro

Haw River

Kitty Hawk

Little Tennessee River

Cherokee

Boone

Hickory

Chapel Hill

Durham

Phelps Lake

Albemarle Sound

Nags Head

Lake Hiwassee

Asheville

Winston Salem

Raleigh

Lake Mattamuskeet

French Broad River

Lake Norman

High Rock Lake

Deep Pee Dee River

Neuse River

New Bern

Pamlico Sound

Hatteras

Charlotte

Ocracoke

Fayetteville

Fort Bragg

Cape Fear River

Camp Lejeune Marine Corps Base

Lake Waccamaw

ATLANTIC OCEAN

N

W E

S

The Tar Heel State

North Carolina is the widest state east of the Mississippi River. It stretches 560 miles (900 kilometers) from sandy beaches in the east through open plains and lush forests to rugged mountains in the west. Still, the state can be crossed by car in less than a day.

North Carolina is bounded by the Appalachian Mountains on one side and by the Atlantic Ocean on the other. The state's northern boundary, which it shares with Virginia, is almost straight. Its southern border, which separates North Carolina from South Carolina and Georgia, looks very bumpy on a map.

North Carolina is divided into one hundred counties. Charlotte, the city with the largest population in the state, is located in Mecklenburg County. Close to 700,000 people live in Charlotte—almost twice as many as live in the second-largest city. Also known as the Queen City, Charlotte is the second largest financial center in the nation. Raleigh, North Carolina's capital city, is located in Wake County, near the center of the state.

With a wide variety of landscapes, North Carolina is a state known for its great beauty. To the east lie the shore and the islands of the Outer

Quick Facts

NORTH CAROLINA BORDERS

North	Virginia
South	South Carolina
	Georgia
East	Atlantic Ocean
West	Tennessee

North Carolina Counties

North Carolina has 100 counties.

Banks. The coastal plain, a flat and often marshy area, is found a little farther inland. In the center of the state, in the broad region called the Piedmont, gently rolling hills are crisscrossed by small rivers and streams. Centuries ago, forests covered the Piedmont. Today, there are fewer trees, but groves still fill the region, even in the area's many cities. To the west, North Carolina grows rugged and wilder. Mountain chains stand tall on the horizon.

Quick Facts

A PIRATE'S NEST
During the late 1600s and early 1700s, many pirates took a liking to the Outer Banks. The islands and coves were ideal for hiding their ships and treasures. Pirates would also chase other ships toward the Outer Banks, forcing them to crash into a shoal. Stories of Blackbeard and other swashbucklers are still told on the islands today.

The Outer Banks

A long and narrow chain of islands lies just off the coast of North Carolina in the Atlantic Ocean. The area, known as the Outer Banks, serves as a barrier that protects the mainland from storms and strong waves. Warm water from the Gulf of Mexico and cold water from Canada mix along North Carolina's shores. These two strong ocean currents, or flows of water, cause these islands to change in size. The streams of water that run between the islands are called channels. The depth of these channels also changes. This makes it hard for boaters to navigate the Outer Banks. Many ships have crashed on the coast—from Spanish galleons full of gold to four-masted schooners. In fact, sailors call the Outer Banks the "Graveyard of the Atlantic." Many lighthouses have been built to guide ships away from treacherous shallow waters, or shoals.

In the days before European settlers came to North Carolina, American Indians known as the Hatteras camped on the Outer Banks islands every summer. They went there to fish, gather clams, catch turtles, and hunt waterfowl. When English settlers first arrived in the New World in the 1580s, they built their earliest settlement on one of the islands. The settlement was called Roanoke,

The Cape Hatteras lighthouse helps guide sailors away from the dangerous waters of North Carolina's Outer Banks.

and the island still bears that name today. The settlement, however, failed.

For many years afterward, few people made their home on the Outer Banks. Brave souls who did establish villages there faced a life of isolation. Then, in the 1950s, the state built a bridge and connected the islands to the mainland. Many people flocked to the Outer Banks to buy land. The U.S. government saw value in the land, too. The National Park Service created two national seashores: Cape Hatteras and Cape Lookout. The islands have nature preserves where wildlife is protected. On the preserves, roads are built only where they will not disturb the wildlife. Outside the preserves, however, private landowners have built many hotels, condominiums, and shopping malls.

Today, many people visit the islands during the warm summer months. They come to enjoy the beach and the ocean and to fish. Bird-watchers visit year-round to see the different seabirds. These include long-legged herons, egrets, ospreys, and a variety of gulls.

The Coast and the Plain Beyond

Several broad shallow sounds, or bays, separate the Outer Banks and North Carolina's mainland. Pamlico Sound is the largest. In some places, waves lapping against the shore have formed tiny harbors. Rivers often flow slowly and form estuaries or deltas as they near the ocean. A place where a river with a broad mouth meets the ocean is called an estuary. There, the fresh water and ocean water blend into a brackish, or slightly salty, mixture. A delta is a flat area where a river breaks into many smaller channels near its mouth. In North Carolina, people use these small waterways to raise, or farm, seafood.

The area near the shore is the coastal plain. The land is often wet and swampy. Ocean tides regularly rise high enough to flood the area. The Great Dismal Swamp covers more than 150 square miles (400 sq km) in the eastern and very northern part of the state plus parts of Virginia. The Great Dismal Swamp National Wildlife Refuge supports many creatures, including otters, deer, salamanders, and poisonous snakes. Grasslands have appeared in other places along the coast. Waterbirds and some alligators make their homes there. In the past, fishers built towns along the coast. Today, more and more retired people have moved to the area, drawn by its quiet and restful pace.

Paddlers wait in the Dismal Swamp Canal to start the 7.5-mile (12-km) trip toward Virginia in North Carolina's annual Paddle for the Border event.

WHERE IS THE WATER?
The sandy hills of the coastal plains look as if they should be near the ocean, but they are actually many miles inland in the area around Fort Bragg. This is because that area was once a shoreline—when dinosaurs still roamed the Earth one hundred million years ago.

Farther inland are stretches of sandy plains and hills that were once covered by longleaf-pine forests. Today, most of the land there has been turned into farms. The soil in this part of the plain is good for growing tobacco, peanuts, soybeans, and sweet potatoes.

The Piedmont

The coastal soil gives way to a region of clay and rock known as the Piedmont. The border between the Piedmont and the coastal plain is called the Fall Line. Along the Fall Line, the land elevation in places is significantly higher in the Piedmont than in the plain. There are cliffs along the Fall Line and waterfalls in the rivers flowing toward the Atlantic. The Piedmont covers nearly half the state. Much of the area has red soil that is rich in clay. This makes it hard to grow a wide range of crops, but one crop that does very well in the region is tobacco. At one time, many decades ago, the Piedmont was a thriving tobacco

The Winston-Salem skyline features the tallest buildings in the Piedmont.

farming region. The area has changed in recent decades. Starting with Charlotte in the south, the state's biggest cities, including Winston-Salem, Greensboro, Raleigh, and Durham, form an arc north and east across the Central Piedmont. Some of the Piedmont's residents still make their living from the land, but most live and work in these large cities and their suburbs. Many have jobs in schools, universities, stores, offices, and factories.

MONADNOCKS
A monadnock is a lone peak or ridge that rises high above the average elevation of the surrounding land. Some of North Carolina's most visited parks include monadnocks called Hanging Rock, Pilot Mountain, and Stone Mountain. Although the geology of the various monadnocks is not always similar, they do share one trait. The rock on the top of a monadnock is better able to resist erosion than the surrounding rocks.

Moving west across the Piedmont, the land rises, reaching as high as 1,500 feet (450 meters) above sea level at the foot of the Blue Ridge Mountains. Hills with round tops, called monadnocks, and long, low ridges are spread across the Piedmont. The area also has some low mountains, such as the Uwharrie. Small rivers and streams cut across the region, offering great spots for rafting, canoeing, and fishing.

The Mountains

Beyond the Piedmont lies North Carolina's mountain region. It includes many different ranges, all of which form part of the huge Appalachian mountain chain that runs from Canada to Alabama. The Appalachians are one of the oldest ranges in the world. Over hundreds of millions of years, its peaks have been worn down by wind, rain, and snow. As a result, they are no longer rough and jagged. Some appear rounded or even flat at the top. Steep valleys and gorges plunge between the peaks. Some of the valleys are laced with sparkling waterfalls.

The Blue Ridge Mountains rise sharply at the western edge of the Piedmont, running northeast to southwest. The U.S. government has built a scenic highway—a road designed to provide great views—through the mountains. The Blue Ridge Parkway is the most visited of all American sites that are managed by the National Park Service. More than 15 million people drive through every year. The region's main city, Asheville, lies near the parkway.

The Blue Ridge Mountains are not one large range; they are made up of many smaller ranges. These include the Black, Bald, Brushy, Great Balsam, Stone, and Unaka mountains. The Black Mountains get their name from the dark green Fraser fir trees that cover them, which make the mountains look almost black. North Carolina's highest peak can be found there. Mount Mitchell, which rises 6,684 feet (2,037 m) above sea level, is the highest peak in the United States east of the Mississippi River. The peak is a part of Mount Mitchell State Park. Founded in 1915, it was North Carolina's first state park.

Beyond the Blue Ridge Mountains lies a broad, high plateau. A plateau is an area of flat land at a high elevation. The Great Smoky Mountains (also known as the "Smokies") sit beyond that plateau on the border of North Carolina and Tennessee. Early English explorers named the Blue Ridge and the Great Smoky mountain ranges after the smoky blue haze that often covers their peaks. In June 1934, a large part of the Smokies was named the Great Smoky Mountains National Park.

The highlight of a visit to Chimney Rock State Park is the view from atop the massive 535-million-year-old stone that gives the park its name.

The beautiful Linville Falls waterfall is a popular stop along the Blue Ridge Parkway. There, rushing water drops 90 feet (27 m) into the steep-walled Linville Gorge below.

Many mountain valleys contain rich, fertile land that is good for farming. In the past, some of the region's forests were cleared for lumber and to make room for people's farms and homes. But many dense forests remain. Spruce and fir evergreens can be found high up in the mountains. Hardwood trees such as chestnuts and tulip poplars are common at lower elevations. In the autumn, the mountains are covered with spectacular colors as the leaves on the trees turn red, gold, orange, and yellow.

North Carolina's Waters

Many rivers, streams, and lakes can be found across North Carolina. Most flow toward the Atlantic. A few of these waterways, most notably the French Broad River, flow west to drain into the Mississippi River. Dams have been built on the Yadkin and Catawba rivers to create hydroelectricity—electricity from waterpower. Some rivers are deep and calm enough for big boats to travel on them. Others are narrower and faster flowing. The Nantahala River is ideal for

The Nantahala River is one of North Carolina's premier whitewater rafting spots.

whitewater rafting. Its name, which means the "land of the noonday sun," reflects the fact that sunlight reaches the floor of its gorge only for a short time each afternoon. The state's largest natural lake, Lake Mattamuskeet near the coast, is a popular spot in the warm months.

Climate

North Carolina is a broad state, made up of different regions at different elevations, and it has a wide variety of weather to match. Overall, the climate in the state is generally mild. Springtime in North Carolina is wet and warm, but the summers can be hot. Changes in altitude affect regional weather the most. In the Piedmont, the humidity, or moisture in the air, can be very high. On many summer days in the center of the state, the temperature can rise to more than 90 degrees Fahrenheit (32 degrees Celsius). In the days before air conditioning, some families living in the Piedmont would close up their houses and spend every July at the shore or at mountain resorts. Fayetteville suffered through the hottest day on the state's records in August 1983 when the temperature reached 110 °F (43 °C). For the most part, it is cooler on the eastern coast and in the mountains to the west.

Temperatures are milder in the fall. With the cooler temperatures, the leaves on many trees begin to change color. The North Carolina hills and forests become beautiful seas of red, orange, and yellow. As winter draws closer, the temperature continues to fall. Winters in the mountains are more severe than in other parts of the state. In January 1985, the temperature dipped to –34 °F (–37 °C) on Mount Mitchell.

The mountain regions usually get enough snow to draw skiers and snowboarders. In the Piedmont and on the coastal plain, there are many winter days when the temperature falls below freezing. Snow does fall, and sometimes blizzards hit, but these regions usually receive little snow.

The state gets a lot of rain throughout the year. The most rain falls in the mountains and along the Atlantic coast. Hurricanes are a threat along the coast. About two strike every year. Some can be disastrous. Hurricane Floyd flooded much of the southeast coast in 1999 and caused thirty-five deaths. Summer is often the wettest season, but it can also be the driest. Through 2007 and 2008, the worst-known drought in the state's history dried reservoirs and sapped crops in the west. Many towns responded with laws to better conserve water.

Wildlife

The variety of land features and the moderate weather make North Carolina an ideal home for a wide range of plants. Many different types of grasses grow on the fields and hills, and three-fifths of the state is covered by forests. The trees that make up these forests include different types of ash, birch, cedar, pine, elm, and maple. Hardwoods such as tupelo and cypress dot the swamps and wetlands. The mountainous regions are filled with fir, spruce, and oak. There are also many wildflowers across the state. Various rhododendrons grow everywhere. In the west, bellwort and other lilies grow alongside white-petaled bloodroot and trillium. Dotted horsemint and swamp mallow grow along the coast.

North Carolina has a wide assortment of animals big and small. Deer, opossums,

Quick Facts

THE ROOTS OF CONSERVATION
North Carolinians have long been concerned about preserving their state's natural resources. The Biltmore Forest School in Asheville was the first forestry school in America. Experts in forestry help people live alongside nature without destroying it. From 1898 to 1913, people attended the Asheville school to learn the science behind nature and how to conserve woodlands.

squirrels, and cottontail rabbits are just some of the mammals that can be found across the state. Someone with a sharp eye may also spot a black bear or a fox.

Swans and terns from colder areas spend their winters along the lakes of eastern North Carolina. Backyard bird feeders may attract Carolina chickadees and other songbirds. There are about twenty kinds of raptors—birds of prey—in the state, including bald eagles and turkey vultures. Another big bird, the wild turkey, roams again across North Carolina's backwoods. This great American bird almost disappeared from the state in the 1970s because of too much hunting and other human activities. Conservation efforts have helped bring wild turkeys back to North Carolina in significant numbers.

Southern leopard frogs, eastern newts, and more than eighty other species of amphibians make their homes in or near the state's waters. These areas are also home to seventy kinds of reptiles, including lizards, snakes, and turtles.

American alligators can be found along the coastal plain. Most of the state's thirty-seven types of snakes stick to land. The eastern box turtle, the state reptile, is the only turtle in North Carolina that lives on dry land.

Many types of waterfowl, including geese, can be found in North Carolina. Some make the state their home; others make it a stop along their migration routes.

North Carolina's waters are also filled with fish. Western mountain streams are perfect for trout and smallmouth bass. The lakes and reservoirs of the Piedmont and coastal plain are full of sunfish, crappies, and perch. These are called "panfish" because they are small enough to fit in a frying pan. Dolphins, marlin, sailfish, and sturgeon can be found in the coastal waters of the Atlantic.

As North Carolina's population has continued to grow, some creatures have had trouble adapting to life near humans. When the population of a type of animal or plant shrinks, that animal or plant is called threatened. If a population becomes extremely small, it is called endangered. In North Carolina, there are more than three dozen types of animals and more than two dozen types of plants that are considered threatened or endangered. Scientists and concerned residents work hard to protect the remaining populations. Laws are passed to prevent people from harming these creatures.

There are more than twenty state natural areas and ten national wildlife refuges in North Carolina. Humans are not allowed to develop the land in these areas, and visitors are limited. This lets the animals and plants thrive in their natural habitats. Breeding programs also help endangered animals. At Topsail Beach, endangered sea turtles such as the leatherback are given a safe place to nest. There is even a hospital to care for injured turtles.

Ghost crabs are a familiar site for visitors to any of North Carolina's many beaches.

Red Maple

The red maple grows wild in the mountains of North Carolina. People across the state also plant these large trees in their yards. The fruit of the red maple looks like a small pair of papery wings. In the fall, the tree's leaves turn brilliant colors.

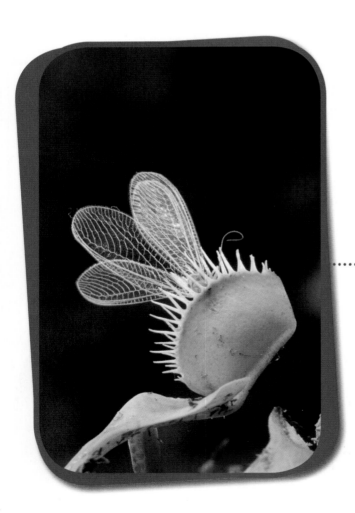

Carolina Rose

The Carolina rose is a bush that can be found growing in open fields and clearings across the mountains and the Piedmont. Its pink flowers bloom in summer and give off a spicy scent.

Venus Flytrap

The Venus flytrap is an insectivore. That means it eats bugs. The plant's bright green leaves are hinged like a trap. Tiny hairs on the leaves sense when an insect brushes against them, and then the leaf snaps shut. The leaf slowly digests the bug and does not open again until it is ready for another meal. Venus flytraps grow naturally in bogs around Wilmington.

Red Wolf

Red wolves once lived across much of the southeast, but many were hunted and killed. Most of their natural habitat was destroyed by human development. As a result, red wolves almost became extinct. The U.S. government started a program in 1987 to return the red wolf to parks in the northeastern corner of the state. Because of these efforts, North Carolina has the world's only population of red wolves in the wild.

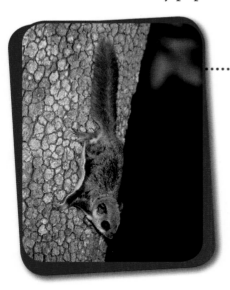

Southern Flying Squirrel

This small mammal does not actually fly. Extra folds of skin stretched between its front and hind legs help the squirrel glide from branch to branch. The squirrel uses its tail, which is long and flattened, to "steer." This squirrel can be brown or gray, has large dark eyes, and usually comes out at night.

Neuse River Waterdog

This spotted salamander is also called the "Carolina mudpuppy." The waterdog makes its home only in the leaves and mud along the Neuse and Tar rivers, where it eats worms and bugs. These giant salamanders can grow up to nine inches (23 centimeters) long. Waterdogs are hard to find because they are nocturnal, which means they are active at night, not during the daytime.

From the Beginning

More than ten thousand years ago, North America's earliest inhabitants settled in what is now North Carolina. The people were nomadic hunters, meaning they followed game animals from place to place. As the years passed, the people became more settled. They set up communities near waterways and forests where game was plentiful. They began planting crops. Archaeologists have discovered evidence of corn crops from about two thousand years ago in the Great Dismal Swamp.

Early Inhabitants

There were at least thirty thousand American Indians living in North Carolina shortly before the arrival of Europeans. The people made up about thirty different tribes. The largest group was the Cherokee, who lived in the western mountains. The Catawbas lived east of the Cherokees, and the Waxhaws, Sugarees, and Saponas lived in the central part of the state. The Tuscaroras were the biggest group in the eastern part of the state. The Hatteras and Chowans were smaller tribes that also lived in this area.

The different tribes had unique traditions, but they shared certain customs. The men hunted and fished, and the women and children took care of the fields. Corn, beans, and squash—known as "the three sisters"—were the most important crops. Some people lived in dwellings called wigwams. Wigwams

Colonist and artist John White made many illustrations that showed the traditions of North Carolina's American Indians. Here, a tribe performs a ceremonial dance.

were made by placing wooden poles in the ground and covering them with bark. The Tuscaroras built longhouses, which were like wigwams only longer. The Cherokees lived in wattle-and-daub dwellings. These structures were made by weaving wood, rivercane, and vines together to create a frame that was then plastered with mud or clay. The roof was made of bark or grass.

When Europeans first came to the area, the American Indians living there greeted them warmly. In fact, if it had not been for the Indians, the Europeans would have quickly starved to death. Before long, however, the colonists' behavior toward the Indians would cause tension between the groups.

European Exploration

Explorer Giovanni da Verrazzano and his crew were the first Europeans believed to reach the coast of North Carolina. The king of France had sent Verrazzano in search of a water route to Asia. The explorer briefly landed on or around Cape Fear in 1524. He then continued northward all the way to the coast of Canada.

In 1540, Spanish explorer Hernando de Soto became the first European to explore the area now known as inland North Carolina. He and his large party of soldiers traveled from what is now Florida up to the Blue Ridge Mountains in search of gold. They reached as far north as present-day Asheville but did not establish settlements. After de Soto died (while exploring farther west), some of his men returned to Spain and reported that they never found any gold. Still, in the thirty years that followed, other Spanish explorers continued to travel north

This illustration shows a meeting between Hernando de Soto and a leader of the Cofitachequi tribe.

from Florida. After that, the Spanish government lost interest in settling the area.

England, on the other hand, became very interested in claiming the area by establishing settlements. In 1584, two English ships approached the Outer Banks in search of a place to anchor. The vessels' captains were sent there by Sir Walter Raleigh. Raleigh was a government official who wanted to help the queen expand the English empire, as well as learn more about the North American coast. When his explorers returned to England with news that they had found an ideal place, he decided to colonize the area. At the time, the region, which was called Virginia, covered present-day Virginia, the Carolinas, and several other states. Raleigh never came to the region, but he paid others to settle there. In the summer of 1585, about one hundred men arrived to establish a colony on Roanoke Island.

The Lost Colony

The island colony of Roanoke was not successful. The first settlers arrived too late to grow their own crops, and they had to rely on the help of local Indians. Relations between the English and the Indians soon soured, though. During a visit to an American Indian village, an Englishman noticed he was missing a silver cup. He said an Indian had stolen it. As punishment, he burned the entire village and the people's corn crops. Within a year of the Englishmen's arrival, tensions began to grow. After English soldiers killed Chief Wingina of the Roanoke tribe, the Indians really began to fear and hate the settlers. They would not help them survive. In fact, many wanted to see them dead. The Englishmen soon returned to England.

Raleigh made a second attempt at colonization in 1587. This time, he persuaded whole families to go to the island. For this trip, John White (who had been part of the earlier expedition) led the group. A total of 110 settlers, including seventeen women and nine children, arrived on Roanoke Island in July. They repaired the cottages that had been built by the earlier settlers and rebuilt an abandoned fort on the northern end of the island. Less than a month after they arrived, White's daughter gave birth to a baby girl. Virginia Dare was the first English child born on American soil.

Soon the colonists realized that they needed more supplies. White took a ship back to England for food, tools, and more settlers. Before leaving Roanoke, he and the settlers agreed that if they decided to move, they would carve a message onto a tree noting where they had gone. They also agreed that if the settlers carved a cross over the message that would indicate that they were in danger at the time of the move.

Fighting between England and Spain prevented White from returning to Roanoke Island until August 1590. When he finally returned, he found the settlement and the fort abandoned. All the colonists had vanished. White found "CRO" scratched onto one tree trunk and "CROATOAN" carved onto another. There was no cross carved at either spot. White thought that the settlers had

The lost settlers of Roanoke left the word "CROATOAN" carved into a tree. They were never found.

gone south to live with the friendly Croatan Indians on Hatteras Island. Bad weather and the war with Spain stopped him from finding out, however. White was forced to give up his search and return to England. Raleigh later sent other parties in search of the missing settlers, but they were never found.

Successful Settlement

Despite its failures at Roanoke, England pushed ahead to settle its Virginia colony (much larger at the time than the modern-day state of Virginia). A settlement called Jamestown prospered about 150 miles (240 km) north of Roanoke, in present-day Virginia. (Jamestown was the first permanent English settlement in North America.) In 1629, King Charles I gave all the land between Albemarle Sound and Spanish Florida to Lord Robert Heath. It was called Carolana in the king's honor (*Carolus* means "Charles" in Latin). The spelling later became Carolina. Heath never developed the territory, but colonists from present-day Virginia began settling the northeastern corner of Carolina by 1660. They had come south looking for fertile land on which to grow crops such as tobacco. At the time, tobacco was so valuable that the crops could be sold for close to their weight in gold. These settlers also brought the first African-American slaves to the region.

This map from the 1600s shows a portion of present-day North Carolina.

In 1663, Charles II gave the land that had belonged to Heath to eight other men. These Lords Proprietors, as they were called, divided the territory into three counties: Albemarle, Clarendon (at Cape Fear), and Craven (in present-day South Carolina). Albemarle County attracted the most new people and quickly formed an assembly, North Carolina's first legislature. By the 1700s, land-hungry colonists were settling to the south and west of Albemarle. Swiss and German Protestants fleeing war in their homelands created New Bern in 1710. The notorious Blackbeard and other pirates haunted the treacherous shoals along the coast, preying on passing ships.

As the Carolina settlements grew, problems arose for the area's American Indian residents. Most colonists, such as those at New Bern, tried to drive the natives away from the coast, making more room for settlements. Some kidnapped and enslaved tribe members. In 1711, the Tuscaroras tried to reassert their power along the Neuse and Pamlico rivers. They killed more than one hundred settlers. The settlers fought back, killing and capturing thousands of Indians. After a treaty was signed in 1715, many Tuscaroras moved out of the region. Others were relocated to reservations.

Following the treaty, a new wave of settlers pushed into the area. Planters came to Cape Fear from South Carolina (which had become a separate colony in 1712). A few had enough slaves to start rice plantations in the area's swampy land. Many more found work harvesting pine tree sap for tar and pitch, which were used by the British Navy to cover ships' hulls.

In 1729, Great Britain's King George II bought most of the land owned by the Lords Proprietors. At the time, about 35,000 people lived in North Carolina, but the size of the population would soon change dramatically. In the 1730s, thousands of Scots and Germans traveled the Great Wagon Road from Pennsylvania, through Virginia's Shenandoah Valley, into the Piedmont. By 1770, there were 200,000 people in the colony. Most were farmers. Only about 5,000 lived in towns.

One thing the colony did lack was a permanent seat of government. The legislature met in different places. Sometimes it assembled in a delegate's home. At other times, it met in a town courthouse. Finally, in 1766, New Bern, located in the eastern part of the colony, was chosen as the colony's capital. A governor's mansion was finished in 1770.

Revolution

Beginning in the 1760s, colonists in North Carolina, as in the other colonies, grew unhappy with British rule. They felt that they were taxed too heavily, and they were angry that they could not represent themselves in the British Parliament that met in London. Colonists who strongly opposed British policies and favored taking action to change

In Their Own Words

[The American Indians] are really better to us than we are to them; they always give us [food] at their Quarters and take care that we are armed against Hunger and Thirst; we do not so by them . . . but let them walk by our Doors Hungry and do not often relieve them.

—From *Lawson's History of North Carolina* (1709)

Construction of St. Philip's Church was completed in 1768. Eight years later, the British burned it down during the American Revolution. The remains of the church (shown here) have been preserved at the Old Brunswick Town State Historic Site.

them became known as patriots. War broke out when patriots and British troops fought at Lexington and Concord in Massachusetts in April 1775—the American Revolution had, in effect, begun.

In February 1776, about 1,000 North Carolina patriots fought 1,600 Scottish Highlanders at Moore's Creek Bridge. The Scots were traveling from Cross Creek (now Fayetteville) to Wilmington, where they planned to join with British troops. After the battle, North Carolina's Provincial Congress decided to support independence for the colonies. With these Halifax Resolves of April 12, 1776, North Carolina became the first colony to vote in favor of breaking away from British rule. Three months later, at the Continental Congress in Philadelphia, North Carolina joined the twelve other colonies in voting in favor of the Declaration of Independence on July 4, 1776.

The American Revolution was a difficult time for the people of North Carolina. Many men and boys joined the Continental Army and fought in the war. Some battles were fought on North Carolina soil. The biggest battle occurred at the town called Guilford Courthouse, now Greensboro, in 1781. North Carolinians who had not joined the army fought to protect their homes from British soldiers and did what they could to support the colonial troops. British general Lord Charles Cornwallis had so much trouble with the people of Charlotte that the city became known as a "hornets' nest." The people of Charlotte were so proud of this that a hornets' nest became a symbol of the city.

The Americans won their independence in 1783. The former colonies were now a new country called the United States. The U.S. Constitution was written in 1787. This was a bold plan to establish a national government with enough power to effectively govern the new nation. North Carolinians believed that the document did not provide enough protection for individuals. They did not ratify (accept) the Constitution until the Bill of Rights was added. The Bill of Rights is made up of the first ten amendments to the Constitution. Among other things,

Militiamen from Maryland fought a bloody battle against the British at Guilford Courthouse on March 15, 1781.

these amendments guarantee Americans freedom of speech and religion, as well as protections from unjust government actions. The amendments also offer certain protections to any citizen who is suspected or accused of a crime.

The people of North Carolina decided it was time to build a new capital city. In 1792, officials purchased 1,000 acres (405 hectares) of land in Wake County, in the center of the state. They decided to name the new capital city Raleigh, after the sponsor of the Roanoke colony.

A New State

North Carolina remained a rural state for most of the nineteenth century. Only Wilmington had more than five thousand people by 1850. Thousands of small farms dotted the Piedmont. There, farmers grew corn, tobacco, and cotton, and they raised livestock. More than half owned five or fewer slaves to help work the land—if they owned any slaves at all. Even though there were fewer slaves in North Carolina than in other Southern states, many residents believed they could not do without slavery. Large plantations were not as common in the state as they were in Virginia or South Carolina, but the number did grow in the period before the Civil War. In the mid–1800s, slaves made up about one-third of North Carolina's population.

Many people left North Carolina for cheaper land farther west in parts of present-day Kentucky and Tennessee. This migration began in the 1760s with pioneers such as Daniel Boone, who had lived on the Yadkin River. Over the next hundred years, hundreds of thousands moved west—including future-presidents Andrew Jackson, James Polk, and Andrew Johnson.

At the time, the Cherokees were already living in the western part of the state, as well as in much of the inland Southeast. In European terms, the Cherokee nation was a very "advanced" civilization. The tribe had a constitution, a court system, and even a newspaper. Between 1777 and 1819, the Cherokees had given up nearly 9,000 square miles (23,000 sq km) of land to the U.S. government. Nevertheless many white Americans believed the Indians were "in the way." By 1839, President Andrew Jackson had forced many Cherokees and other American Indians in the Southeast to move west into the Oklahoma Territory. The difficult journey became known as the Trial of Tears.

One big draw to North Carolina during this time was the discovery of gold at Little Meadow Creek in Cabarrus County in 1799. In the first half of the 1800s, the southern Piedmont became the site of the nation's first gold rush. The money made from gold mining was second only to that made from agriculture in the state.

Every year, people such as this young boy gather together to participate in the Trail of Tears Re-enactment Walk.

THE TRAIL OF TEARS

Quick Facts

As part of President Andrew Jackson's Indian removal policy, the Cherokee nation was made to give up all of its land east of the Mississippi River. In 1838 and 1839, about 15,000 people were forced to walk to present-day Oklahoma. Hunger, disease, and exhaustion claimed the lives of 4,000 Cherokees, who called the march *Nunna dual Tsyny*—"The Trail Where They Cried." This tragic journey is now commonly referred to as the Trail of Tears.

MAKING A HOMEMADE DOLL

Historians have found that very old North Carolina homes often hold small historical treasures, such as a simple handmade doll. A toy like this may have belonged to a child who lived in the house more than 150 years ago. When store-bought goods were hard to come by, parents sometimes made toys for their children using household items. You can make a similar doll by following these instructions.

WHAT YOU NEED

Pencil with eraser

Piece of paper at least 8 $\frac{1}{2}$ by 11 inches (22 by 28 cm)

Scissors

Two pieces of felt, at least 8 $\frac{1}{2}$ by 11 inches (22 by 28 cm)

Sewing pins

Ballpoint pen

Small stapler

18 square inches (116 sq cm) of polyester or cotton batting cut into pieces, or two or three pairs of old pantyhose

One piece of narrow ribbon, about 2 feet (60 cm) long

With the pencil, draw the outline of the doll's body on the paper. Be sure to make the doll large enough so that you will not have problems cutting it out and putting it together. The bottom of the body should line up with the bottom of the paper. Cut out the doll using the line as your guide. Stack one piece of felt on top of the other and pin the doll cutout on top.

Trace the outline of the doll onto the felt using the ballpoint pen. Remove the paper.

Pin the two pieces of felt together and cut around your tracing. Staple all the edges except the bottom. (Make sure to staple the felt as close to the outside edge as possible.) Stuff the doll with the batting or pantyhose and then staple the bottom closed.

Draw a face on the doll with the ballpoint pen and tie the ribbon around its neck. Enjoy your old-fashioned homemade doll!

The Civil War Era

By the 1850s, tensions were rising between the Northern and Southern states. Most Northern states did not have economies that relied as much on agriculture—and especially on large plantations—as did the South. As a result, the North did not need slaves. Many Northern states had abolished (or put an end to) slavery. Many people living in the North felt that slavery should be outlawed throughout the nation. Besides disagreeing with the North's stand on slavery, many Southern states were unhappy with the federal government. They felt that the states were not given enough rights and that the U.S. government had too much control.

The nation quickly divided after Abraham Lincoln, an antislavery Republican, was elected president in 1860. By March 1861, seven Southern states had seceded from (or left) the United States (also called the Union at that time) and formed the Confederate States of America (CSA). Other states followed. On May 20, 1861, North Carolina became the eleventh, and final, Southern state to secede from the Union.

North Carolina supplied 125,000 men to the Confederate army. Tens of thousands of them died during the war. Many important Civil War events occurred in North Carolina, including one of the Confederacy's final stands. In late March 1865, Confederate general Joseph E. Johnston led his forces against Union general William T. Sherman at the bloody Battle of Bentonville. Nearly 5,000 men died. Two weeks later, Confederate general Robert E. Lee surrendered his army at Appomattox Court House in Virginia. Johnston surrendered his army of Confederate troops to Sherman near Durham on April 26, 1865. After four years of bloody fighting, the Civil War was over. The CSA had been defeated, and the South was again part of the United States.

The states of the former Confederacy were at first under U.S. military control. They had to meet several requirements before being allowed to reenter the Union as states. Each had to write a new state constitution and ratify the Thirteenth, Fourteenth, and Fifteenth amendments to the U.S. Constitution. (The Thirteenth

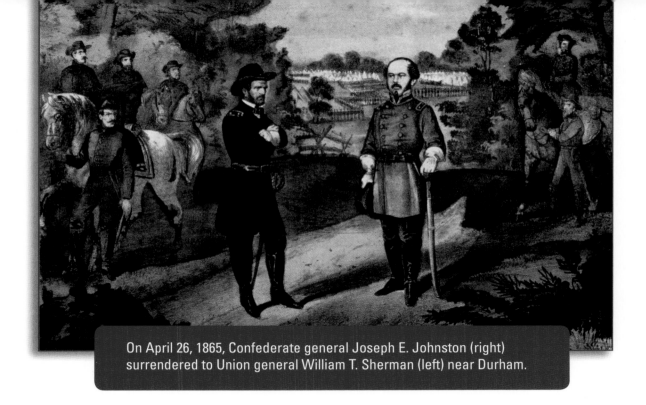

On April 26, 1865, Confederate general Joseph E. Johnston (right) surrendered to Union general William T. Sherman (left) near Durham.

Amendment abolished slavery nationwide; the Fourteenth guaranteed all people equal protection under the law; and the Fifteenth gave black men the right to vote.) After meeting the necessary requirements, North Carolina was readmitted to the Union as a state in 1868.

The Late 1800s

In the decades after the Civil War, agriculture continued to be important in North Carolina. Newly completed railroads allowed farmers to send their crops across the state and throughout the entire nation. Many chose to grow what are known as cash crops, such as cotton and tobacco, which sold for more money than such food staples as corn and wheat.

Most farmers in the area, especially former slaves, did not own their land. They were sharecroppers. Under this system, a person farmed a parcel of land, and the resulting crops were divided, or shared, between the worker and the landowner. Most landowners took advantage of this arrangement and created a system that kept sharecroppers in poverty.

After the Civil War, many former-slaves worked as sharecroppers. Here, a cropper plows a cotton field.

Mills to turn cotton into cloth and tobacco into cigarettes became other important sources for jobs. The owners often created "mill towns" around the factories, where workers and their families lived. Many children labored alongside their parents in the mills. Both children and adults often worked long hours in dangerous conditions for low pay.

Into the Twentieth Century

The beginning of the twentieth century was a very innovative time in the United States. On December 17, 1903, a pair of brothers, Wilbur and Orville Wright, made the world's first controlled, engine-powered airplane flights in North Carolina. For years, the Wright brothers had been trying to build a heavier-than-air plane that they could steer and that had an engine. Orville Wright's first, 120-foot (37-m) flight at Kill Devil Hill near Kitty Hawk, on the coast of North Carolina, lasted only twelve seconds, but it is now regarded as one of the greatest events in human history. The brothers made three other flights the same day.

North Carolina's manufacturing industries thrived thanks to innovators, too. In New Bern, the pharmacist Caleb D. Bradham created a tasty cola, "Brad's Drink." It became Pepsi in 1898. James B. Duke made a fortune after he licensed from its inventor the right to use the first automated cigarette-making machine at Duke's American Tobacco Company. Later, in the 1920s, Duke used some of his money to establish Duke University. Today, Duke is one of the nation's leading universities, respected for both its academics and its athletics.

Many Americans lost their jobs after the Great Depression started in 1929. During these very hard economic times, which continued through the 1930s, many factories in North Carolina closed down. Many families moved to cities such as Durham, where a few tobacco factories and Duke University could still provide some jobs. Other families left the state and moved west in search of work. President Franklin D. Roosevelt began several new programs

Wilbur Wright (above) and his brother Orville first took to the air at Kill Devil Hill on the North Carolina coast.

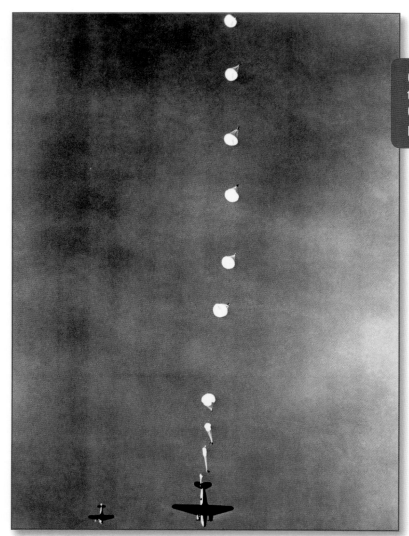

to help Americans get back to work. The U.S. government's Works Progress Administration (WPA) hired millions of people for construction projects and other kinds of work. In North Carolina, some of these workers built the Blue Ridge Parkway, as well as schools, parks, and many other facilities that are still used today.

The Great Depression ended as the United States entered World War II in 1941. North Carolina became a major training center for soldiers. Fort Bragg, near Fayetteville, grew to handle 159,000 personnel. Marines that trained on the beaches at Camp Lejeune went on to fight in many important battles in the Pacific. When the men of North Carolina signed up to fight in the war, women took their places in the factories. The state's textile factories made North Carolina the largest manufacturer of army uniforms of any state in the country.

Growing Pains

After World War II ended in 1945, African-American soldiers returned home to face a sad reality. Despite their service to their country, they—and other African

Americans—were still being treated like second-class citizens. Since the end of the nineteenth century, segregation laws in North Carolina, and in other states, had prevented African Americans from doing many of the things that white citizens took for granted. Under these "Jim Crow" laws, black people had to attend separate schools and could not sit with, travel with, or eat with whites in public places such as movie theaters, trains, and restaurants. Without exception, the schools and facilities designated "colored only" were far inferior to those used by whites.

In the 1950s and 1960s, African Americans in North Carolina played a key role in the growing civil rights movement. They were fighting for laws that would outlaw discrimination based on race. On February 1, 1960, four African-American college students entered a Woolworth's store in Greensboro and sat at the lunch counter. At that time, black people were not allowed to sit at the

In North Carolina, as in other Southern states, segregation was strictly enforced. This boy is drinking from a "colored" water fountain outside the county courthouse in Halifax.

counter. The waitress, and then the store manager, refused to serve the young men. Still, they stayed in their seats. They did not leave until Woolworth's closed for the night. They returned the next day and for days after that, each day accompanied by more and more fellow protesters. This peaceful protest inspired other similar demonstrations, called sit-ins, in other states. By July 1960, the Woolworth Company agreed to integrate the lunch counter, allowing whites and blacks to sit together. Eventually, by the mid–1960s, Congress passed laws intended to end nationwide racial discrimination in many areas of public life.

Looking Forward

In the later decades of the twentieth century and the beginning of the twenty-first, North Carolina experienced rapid growth. The state's population went from 5 million in 1970 to 9 million by 2007. Many new jobs were created in banking and finance and in high-tech industries, especially in the region that became known as the Research Triangle. The area includes the cities of Raleigh, Durham, and Chapel Hill and such leading universities as Duke and the University of North Carolina at Chapel Hill.

The state has attempted to balance growth with protection of its environment and heritage. For years, North Carolina's industries had been polluting the state's rivers. Citizens went to the polls and voted in favor of clean-water projects to help clean up the state's waterways. Durham and other cities started special programs to save their historic buildings while still encouraging business leaders to build new factories and office buildings. Today, many of North Carolina's cities are featured on national lists of the best places to live or work.

Important Dates

★ **8000 BCE** American Indian groups enter what is now North Carolina.

★ **1524** Explorer Giovanni da Verrazzano becomes the first European to see the coast of present-day North Carolina.

★ **1540** Explorer Hernando de Soto and his men explore the southern part of what is called North Carolina today.

★ **1584** Sir Walter Raleigh sends several ships carrying settlers to Roanoke Island—the New World's first English colony.

★ **1776** Colonists in North Carolina create the Halifax Resolves, becoming the first colony to vote in favor of breaking from British rule.

★ **1789** North Carolina becomes the twelfth state to ratify the U.S. Constitution.

★ **1861–1865** The Civil War is fought. North Carolina participates as part of the Confederate States of America.

★ **1868** North Carolina is readmitted as a state to the United States.

★ **1903** The Wright brothers' airplane flights make history.

★ **1917** Camp Bragg is founded as an artillery training school.

★ **1937** North Carolina becomes the first state to establish a soil and water conservation district to help farmers preserve resources and reuse their land.

★ **1954** Hurricane Hazel batters the North Carolina coast. It is the most destructive storm in the state's history up to that time.

★ **1960** A sit-in protesting segregation begins at a Woolworth's lunch counter in Greensboro.

★ **1982** Freshman Michael Jordan makes "the shot," giving the UNC men's basketball team the NCAA championship win over Georgetown University.

★ **1999** Hurricane Floyd causes dozens of deaths and billions of dollars' worth of damage in North Carolina, becoming the most destructive hurricane to hit the state.

★ **2009** Beverly Perdue becomes North Carolina's first female governor.

The People

For centuries, people have traveled to North Carolina in search of a better life. When North Carolina first became a colony, almost all of its settlers came from England or Scotland. There were also smaller numbers of people from elsewhere in Europe. In the seventeenth century, Africans were brought to North Carolina as slaves. Some African-American families in North Carolina are descended from these slaves. Other African Americans in the state came from other states or other countries.

Many immigrants also arrived in colonial North Carolina from Ireland and Germany. In 1752, several hundred Moravians emigrated from what is now the Czech Republic. They came in search of religious freedom. After the American Revolution, settlers represented a wider variety of European countries, including France, Norway, Sweden, the Netherlands, and Italy. All these different ethnic groups

Quick Facts

AWOOOO!
In the mountains in the days before telephones, neighbors who lived far apart used a "distress holler" in times of emergency. This holler was a long, high call similar to a yodel. According to Leonard Emanuel, who was named National Hollerin' Champion in 1971, hollers helped when children were lost, men were drowning, or houses were on fire.

Children from many diverse cultures call North Carolina home.

made their own mark on North Carolina. They brought with them their own foods and special traditions, including music, dance, and celebrations.

Some people whose English and Irish ancestors settled on the Outer Banks long ago retain a distinctive dialect, or variety of language. One trait of this "Banker" speech comes from the speakers' keeping their lips close together when they speak. They make "i" sound like "oi," so "the toid is hoigh" is how they say, "the tide is high." The dialect also uses words not commonly heard in the rest of the country. During the past few decades, it has become easier to reach many of these islands. Hearing outsiders' speech has reduced Outer Bankers' use of dialect.

The First Residents

Only about one percent of North Carolina's population is American Indian. Still, North Carolina has the largest population of Indians east of the Mississippi River. Some live on farms or in towns and cities across the state. Others choose to live a more traditional life on reservations. Most of the American Indians in the state are Lumbees or Cherokees. The Lumbees have lived for centuries

This young Lumbee boy is dressed in the traditional clothing of his people.

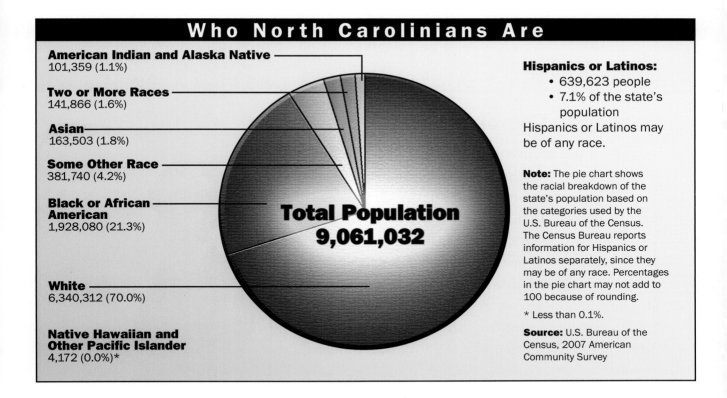

Who North Carolinians Are

American Indian and Alaska Native
101,359 (1.1%)

Two or More Races
141,866 (1.6%)

Asian
163,503 (1.8%)

Some Other Race
381,740 (4.2%)

Black or African American
1,928,080 (21.3%)

White
6,340,312 (70.0%)

Native Hawaiian and Other Pacific Islander
4,172 (0.0%)*

Total Population 9,061,032

Hispanics or Latinos:
- 639,623 people
- 7.1% of the state's population

Hispanics or Latinos may be of any race.

Note: The pie chart shows the racial breakdown of the state's population based on the categories used by the U.S. Bureau of the Census. The Census Bureau reports information for Hispanics or Latinos separately, since they may be of any race. Percentages in the pie chart may not add to 100 because of rounding.

* Less than 0.1%.

Source: U.S. Bureau of the Census, 2007 American Community Survey

in what is now Robeson County. They have been the driving force behind many important regional improvements, including the founding of the state university at Pembroke in 1887. Many Cherokees who live near the Great Smoky Mountains are descendants of those who managed to stay behind after the tribe was forced west along the Trail of Tears. Other American Indian groups in the state include the Coharies, the Haliwa-Saponis, the Meherrins, the Occaneechi Band, the Sappony, and the Waccamaw Siouans.

Through museums, cultural centers, festivals, and powwows, North Carolina's American Indians keep their culture and traditions alive. The Oconaluftee Indian Village, in the western part of the state, shows what everyday life was like for the Cherokees in 1750. Guides teach visitors about Cherokee culture. People in the village also demonstrate traditional activities such as building canoes, preparing food, and making pottery. This is just one of the many ways American Indians in North Carolina share their history and culture with others.

Sequoyah: Cherokee Leader

Sequoyah was a Cherokee Indian born around 1776 in an area of North Carolina that is now part of Tennessee. In those days, the Cherokees had a complex language but no system of writing. Sequoyah wanted his people to be able to create written records of events. He also thought Cherokee soldiers would like to write home to their families. In 1809, Sequoyah began inventing an alphabet of letters for all the sounds of the Cherokee language. He completed his project in 1821. Within months, thousands of Cherokees could write and read their language. As a great honor, Sequoyah was awarded a silver medal by the Cherokee Nation.

Billy Graham: Evangelist

North Carolina native Billy Graham was born in 1918 and raised outside Charlotte. Graham achieved great prominence as an evangelist, someone who teaches and spreads Christianity to others. In the 1940s, he began to host a radio program and hold rallies. During the next fifty years, he traveled all over the United States and around the world.

Earl Scruggs: Musician

Earl Scruggs was born in the mountains of Cleveland County in 1924. As a young man, he joined a band that toured all over the country. He and Lester Flatt later started their own band, called the Foggy Mountain Boys. They had many big hits in the 1960s. Scruggs is considered to be one of the greatest bluegrass musicians and banjo players of all time. In 1985, he was inducted into the Country Music Hall of Fame.

Dale Earnhardt and Dale Earnhardt Jr.: NASCAR Drivers

Racing legend Dale Earnhardt was born in Kannapolis in 1951. He competed in his first auto race in Charlotte in 1975 and spent the next twenty-seven years racking up an impressive list of wins and awards. Earnhardt, who was listed as one of NASCAR's fifty greatest drivers, died tragically as a result of a crash in the final lap of the 2001 Daytona 500. His son, Dale Jr., carries on the family tradition and continues to race in the NASCAR Sprint Cup series.

Michael Jordan: Athlete

Michael Jordan was born in New York City in 1963, but he was raised and educated in Wilmington. Jordan became a basketball star while attending the University of North Carolina (UNC). In the NBA, he led the Chicago Bulls to six championships and set several scoring records. He is widely considered one of the best players of all time. Jordan was so proud of UNC that he wore his college uniform shorts beneath his Bulls uniform in every game for good luck.

Chris Daughtry: Singer

Chris Daughtry, who was born in 1979 in Roanoke Rapids, first gained national attention in 2006 as a contestant on Fox TV's *American Idol*. Although the singer did not win the competition, his television appearances quickly led to success. As frontman for the alternative rock band Daughtry, Chris saw his debut album sell more than one million copies in just five weeks, making it the fastest-selling debut rock album ever. When Daughtry released his second album in 2009, he became the only *Idol* contestant to score two successive number one albums.

Country Life and City Life

In the past, one thing most North Carolinians had in common was that they lived in the country or in very small towns. Recently, however, that has changed. Today, more than half the population lives in cities or suburbs.

North Carolina's cities have grown rapidly in the past few decades. Charlotte is officially the largest city, with a population of roughly 675,000. Almost twice as many people live in the city's suburbs.

Three of North Carolina's other major cities—Raleigh, Chapel Hill, and Durham—are each much smaller than Charlotte. Still, they are located close enough to each other to form a large, overlapping area of suburbs, neighborhoods, and urban centers. More than 1.5 million people live there. Between Raleigh and Durham is an area called Research Triangle Park. Cary is at its center. The park was specifically planned as a place for high-tech companies to operate. Raleigh, as the state capital, has many government buildings and

Charlotte, North Carolina's largest city, is also a major financial center.

The University of North Carolina at Chapel Hill first opened to students on January 15, 1795. Manning Hall (above) is a centerpiece of the university's School of Information and Library Science.

beautiful museums. Durham is home to Duke University and many medical research groups. One campus of the University of North Carolina is located in Chapel Hill, which is a city of gardens and quiet neighborhoods filled with old houses. Farther west, the Piedmont Triad of Greensboro, Winston-Salem, and High Point has its own important educational institutions and museums.

Both the eastern and the western sections of the state have smaller populations than the middle. While there are a few coastal cities, such as Wilmington and Jacksonville, farms are still more common in the region. The few towns in the Outer Banks, such as Nags Head, have small populations after their many visitors depart at the end of the summer. Along the shore, most towns have no more than a few thousand residents. Many of these places have historic houses and two-lane roads that wind through fields, swamps, and pine tree groves.

With more than 3,375 miles (5,430 km) of shoreline (including offshore islands), North Carolina is a beach lover's paradise.

In the mountains to the west, the towns tend to be small. Some, such as Mortimer, are virtually ghost towns, places that were abandoned when a railroad line or a factory was closed down. Other towns, such as Boone, are thriving. Asheville, nestled among the Blue Ridge Mountains, has grown to become the biggest city in western North Carolina.

Regardless of where they live, many North Carolinians share the same concerns. When the state or the country faces tough economic times, individuals and families struggle to provide for themselves—especially in areas where jobs are hard to find. Government programs do help the unemployed and the needy, but sometimes this is not enough. State leaders and concerned citizens are working together to find ways to help create more jobs and provide assistance to those who need it. Across the state, the quality of education remains an important issue. Children make up about one-quarter of the state's population, and most of them attend the state's public schools.

Fun in North Carolina

Lots of North Carolinians head outdoors when they have free time. Many avid hunters live in the state, as do people who love to catch trout in the mountains or bluefish in the ocean. In the winter, skiers head to High Country slopes. Hikers, campers, and bird-watchers especially enjoy North Carolina's state parks. The National Park Service cares for two national seashores, along with the Great Smoky Mountains National Park (located partly in North Carolina and partly in Tennessee), the Blue Ridge Parkway, and many other national points of interest in the state.

Great Smoky Mountains National Park is America's most-visited national park.

Thousands of visitors come to North Carolina each year. One popular attraction out west is the Biltmore Estate in Asheville. The grounds were designed by Frederick Law Olmsted, who is known as the founder of American landscape architecture. With 250 rooms, the estate is the biggest private home

The 8,000-acre (3,250-ha) Biltmore Estate, which includes the house and gardens, a winery, and a farm, is a popular tourist destination. Visitors can also enjoy biking, hiking, horseback riding, and water sports.

in the United States. At Asheboro's North Carolina Zoo, more than a thousand animals are allowed to wander across 500 acres (202 ha) of land. The Carowinds theme park outside Charlotte is a great spot for thrill seekers. It has more than a dozen roller coasters, including the Carolina Cyclone.

North Carolinians are big sports fans. The golf course at Pinehurst Resort is considered one of the greatest in the world. Stock car racing was pioneered in Charlotte. The city and its Motor Speedway are the home of NASCAR. Many racecar drivers live and practice nearby. Famed driving families like the Earnhardts and Pettys call the state home. The state's NFL football team, the Carolina Panthers, plays in Charlotte, too. Nearby, U.S. Olympians train at the U.S. National Whitewater Center. Raleigh's NHL team, the Carolina Hurricanes, won back-to-back Stanley Cup championships in 2005 and 2006.

Basketball is especially popular in North Carolina. Charlotte is home to the NBA Bobcats, the team that replaced the Hornets when they moved to New Orleans in 2002. The state also has world-class college teams. Duke's Blue Devils and UNC's Tar Heels are well known for their rivalry. In 2009, the Tar Heels became the first men's college basketball team to win 100 NCAA tournament games. The Durham Bulls is a minor-league baseball team so colorful that it inspired a movie, *Bull Durham* (1988).

A State for All Ages

Not only does North Carolina have a large population of young people, it also has a large number of senior citizens. Almost one-eighth of the state's population is older than sixty-five. Retired people move to North Carolina for the state's outstanding scenery, mild climate, and many fun things to do.

The competition between the Duke Blue Devils and the North Carolina Tar Heels has been called one of the most intense rivalries in all of sports.

Calendar of Events

★ Azalea Festival

Every spring, when Wilmington's gardens bloom with colorful azalea flowers, thousands flock to the city for the Azalea Festival. Visitors can also enjoy a parade and a street fair, as well as art shows and a tour of local homes.

★ Grifton Shad Festival

Each April, the tiny town of Grifton hosts a celebration honoring the shad, a small fish that lives in the local creek. People come to hear live music, watch cloggers and other dancers, and listen to the outrageous fibs told in the lying competition.

★ The Coca-Cola 600 Auto Race

The longest NASCAR race is also a fan favorite. Every Memorial Day weekend, thousands flock to Charlotte's Motor Speedway to watch stock cars zoom around the track 400 times at speeds upwards of 190 miles per hour (305 km per hr).

★ National Hollerin' Contest

In the days before the telephone, mountain people hollered to their neighbors when they had a message to pass along. Every June, the town of Spivey's Corner is filled with people who have come to compete in the annual National Hollerin' Contest.

★ The Highland Games and Gathering o' Scottish Clans

In July, North Carolinians come to Grandfather Mountain to celebrate their state's Scottish heritage. They enjoy bagpipe music, dancing, food, costumes, and sports such as wrestling and the caber toss. In this event,

athletes throw a huge log that is about 20 feet (6 m) long and weighs about 120 pounds (55 kg).

★ The Mountain Dance and Folk Festival

The first weekend in August, mountain musicians and dancers meet in Asheville. For three evenings "along about sundown" square dancers strut their stuff while balladeers sing tales and mountain musicians strum away.

★ Mule Days

Many North Carolinians never miss Mule Days, held in Benson on the last weekend in September. Hundreds of horses, buggies, and mules from across the world parade through the streets. The weekend also includes carnival rides, mule races, and a rodeo.

★ Cherokee Indian Fair

With autumn comes the Cherokee Indian Fair in Cherokee. There are plenty of typical fair events, such as fireworks and a parade. But the Cherokees also provide traditional entertainment, including stomp dancing and blowgun competitions.

★ Lexington Barbecue Festival

Lexington bills itself as the "Barbecue Capital of the World." Every October, thousands of visitors flock to this festival to enjoy pork barbecue served with the region's signature red slaw, which is made with ketchup instead of mayonnaise.

★ Tryon Palace Christmas Candlelight

New Bern's grandest home steps back in time for the holidays. Visitors can take candlelight tours and enjoy performances by jugglers, acrobats, and sword swallowers. Outside, a band plays fifes and drums. The evening ends with a traditional 1700s fireworks display.

How the Government Works

Governments at several different levels serve North Carolinians. Locally elected officials such as a mayor and members of a city council pass and enforce laws in bigger towns and cities. These laws address such local issues as what types of buildings and businesses can be built near people's homes. Local governments are also in charge of a town or city's police force.

Each of North Carolina's one hundred counties has a government, too. In North Carolina, the law states that every county must have its own elected board of commissioners. The county commissioners choose a county manager. The commissioners' main jobs are to oversee education as well as health and social services. Smaller communities are often unincorporated. This means that the county provides police and other services.

North Carolina is represented in the U.S. Congress in Washington, D.C. Like all other states, it sends two senators to the U.S. Senate. As of 2010,

Quick Facts

THE BIGGEST COUNTIES
Robeson County, located in the Piedmont, is the biggest county in the state. It covers 949 square miles (2,458 sq km) of land. To the west in the hills, Mecklenburg County, with Charlotte as its county seat, is the most populated. About 890,000 people lived in this county as of 2008.

The State Capitol at Raleigh is a National Historic Landmark.

Branches of Government

EXECUTIVE ★ ★ ★ ★ ★ ★ ★ ★ ★

The people of North Carolina elect a governor and lieutenant governor every four years. The governor, who can serve no more than two terms in a row, is the head of the state and signs bills into law—or can reject bills—after the state legislature passes them.

LEGISLATIVE ★ ★ ★ ★ ★ ★ ★ ★

The state legislature is called the general assembly. The general assembly makes the state's laws. It is bicameral, meaning it has two parts (called chambers)—the senate and the house of representatives. There are 50 state senators and 120 state representatives. They are all elected for two-year terms. The lieutenant governor is the president of the senate.

JUDICIAL ★ ★ ★ ★ ★ ★ ★ ★ ★

The judicial branch enforces and interprets the state's laws. Criminal cases and civil cases (disputes between individuals or companies) generally start in a district court if they are minor or in a superior court if they involve more serious crimes or larger amounts of money. Decisions of a district or superior court can be challenged (or appealed) in the court of appeals. Some especially complicated or important cases can be further appealed to the state's highest court, the supreme court. The supreme court can decide whether an earlier judge was wrong or a state law does not agree with the state constitution. The supreme court has a chief justice and six associate justices. Most judges are elected to eight-year terms. The state's district court judges are elected every four years.

North Carolina had thirteen members in the U.S. House of Representatives. Voters in each of the state's congressional districts elect one representative for their district every two years. Statewide elections determine the senators, who serve six-year terms.

State Government

Raleigh, North Carolina's capital, is home to the state government. The governor heads the government's executive branch. The lieutenant governor and eight other elected officials form a Council of State that advises and works with the governor. The governor appoints other high-level officials, including the heads of various departments. The governor and other state officials oversee such aspects of life in the state as transportation, education, and commerce.

The house of representatives chamber shown here was used by state legislators from 1840 to 1961.

The state legislature, which passes the state's laws, is called the general assembly. It starts a new session every year. During odd-numbered years, the assembly holds a "long" session, meeting for about six months starting in January. In the following even-numbered year, the assembly meets for a shorter session of about six to ten weeks. When the general assembly is meeting, Raleigh is a busy place. That is because officials, citizens, and lobbyists—people who represent the interests of a certain industry or group—come to see the legislators and attend the legislative sessions.

How a Bill Becomes a Law

North Carolina's state laws start out as bills (a bill is a proposed law). Sometimes a citizen has an idea for a new law and contacts his or her state senator or representative to suggest it. Other times, state representatives, senators, or members of their staffs come up with an idea. The governor or another state official may also propose a bill to the general assembly.

To start the lawmaking process, a member of the state's general assembly introduces the bill into the state house of representatives or senate. After the bill's title is read out loud, it is assigned a number and sent to a committee that looks closely into every aspect of the bill. The committee discusses the positive and negative aspects of the bill. If necessary, the committee does research, and it may make changes to, or amend, the bill. Any member of the assembly may also suggest changes. If the committee approves the bill, it is then discussed by the entire state senate or house of representatives, depending upon where it was first introduced. Sometimes it is amended again.

If the members vote in favor of the bill, it is sent to the other chamber of the general assembly, which follows the same process. If its members vote in favor of the bill but make changes to it, they send it back to the first chamber for another vote. If the first chamber does not approve of the changes, or makes further changes to the bill, it is sent to a committee containing members of both chambers to work out the differences between the two versions. Ultimately, both chambers most approve the exact same version of a bill.

Most bills that are approved by both houses in the general assembly then go to the governor. He or she can sign it, in which case it becomes law. The governor can also decide to take no action and allow the bill to become law without his or her signature. The governor also has the right to veto, or reject, the bill. When this happens, the bill goes back to the general assembly for yet another vote. If at least three-fifths of the members in each house vote for the bill, it becomes a law. This is called overriding the governor's veto.

Getting Involved

Throughout the state's history, North Carolinians have taken an active part in their government. For example, concerned citizens have called attention to issues associated with such aspects of life in the state as the environment, education, and crime. A lot of the state's legislation is shaped by the voice of the people.

Governor Beverly Perdue and a friend take part in Plant a Row for the Hungry, which helps bring healthful food to hungry families in Raleigh, Durham, and Chapel Hill.

Making a Living

For most of its history, North Carolina was a farm state. Today, however, the agriculture industry accounts for less than 2 percent of the state's total jobs. There are about 52,000 farms in the state. Many farmers raise livestock such as hogs, cattle, and poultry. Farmers in the Piedmont raise a seventh of America's turkeys in addition to millions of chickens and billions of eggs. Beginning in the 1990s, the southeast counties became a center for hog farming. Farms in North Carolina raise more pigs than those in any other state but Iowa.

North Carolina remains the largest producer of tobacco in the United States. Tobacco is still the state's most valuable crop, even though the annual harvest continues to shrink as more people become aware of the health problems caused by smoking. More than a third of jobs in the American tobacco industry are based in North Carolina. The state is also a leading producer of Christmas trees, sweet potatoes, and strawberries.

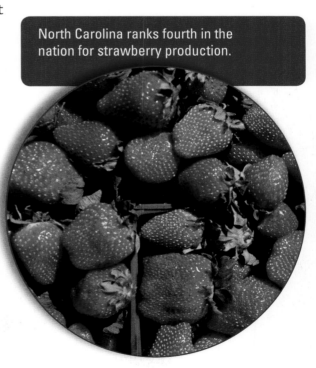

North Carolina ranks fourth in the nation for strawberry production.

A factory worker in Greensboro inspects fabric to be used inside cars. The textile industry is an important part of North Carolina's economy.

RECIPE FOR SWEET POTATO PIE

Sweet potatoes are an important North Carolina crop. This recipe shows you how to use them in a simple, tasty dessert. You will need to use the oven, so ask an adult for help.

WHAT YOU NEED

2 $\frac{1}{2}$ cups (567 grams) cooked mashed sweet potatoes

1 cup (237 milliliters) evaporated milk

2 large eggs

1 $\frac{1}{4}$ cup (248 g) granulated sugar

$\frac{1}{2}$ cup (113 g) butter

$\frac{1}{2}$ teaspoon (2 g) cinnamon

1 $\frac{1}{2}$ teaspoon (7 ml) vanilla extract

9 inch (23 cm) frozen piecrust

Preheat the oven to 425 °F (220 °C).

Place all the ingredients in a large bowl and beat with an electric mixer until well blended. Pour the mixture into the piecrust.

Bake the pie for ten minutes, and then reduce the heat to 350 °F (175 °C). Bake for about 55 minutes longer, or until a knife inserted into the center of the pie comes out clean.

Allow the pie to cool after baking and then ask an adult to help you slice it and serve it. Serve each slice with a dollop of whipped cream, if desired.

The Charlotte Mint was in operation from 1838 until 1861. During the Civil War, it was turned into a Confederate headquarters and hospital.

Mining

Gold was first found in North Carolina in 1799. But it was not until 1842, when the first vertical mine shaft was dug, that miners found large amounts of this precious metal. (A vertical mine shaft is one in which a tunnel is dug from the ground straight down into the earth. Other shafts may be dug into the side of a mountain and head straight back.) One year later, a prospector named Peter Earnhardt discovered the richest and deepest gold mine east of the Mississippi River. The growth of mining in North Carolina prompted the U.S. government to build a mint in Charlotte. A mint is a place where coins are manufactured. Today, a museum sits on the site of the original mint.

Workers & Industries

Industry	Number of People Working in That Industry	Percentage of All Workers Who Are Working in That Industry
Education and health care	921,355	21.8%
Wholesale and retail businesses	622,393	14.7%
Manufacturing	573,575	13.6%
Publishing, media, entertainment, hotels, and restaurants	431,396	10.2%
Professionals, scientists, and managers	391,357	9.3%
Construction	381,071	9.0%
Banking and finance, insurance, and real estate	283,247	6.7%
Other services	195,629	4.6%
Transportation and public utilities	192,529	4.6%
Government	173,535	4.1%
Farming, fishing, forestry, and mining	61,737	1.5%
Totals	**4,227,824**	**100%**

Notes: Figures above do not include people in the armed forces. "Professionals" includes people such as doctors and lawyers. Percentages may not add to 100 because of rounding.

Source: U.S. Bureau of the Census, 2007 estimates

Gold mining is no longer common in the state, but other products are mined from the land. During the eighteenth century, North Carolinians started making bricks and tiles from the red clay found in the Piedmont. At that time, people often used fireplaces and wood stoves to heat their homes. Clay bricks and tiles were needed for the chimneys and roofs because the clay would

not catch fire from a stray spark. Today, North Carolinians mine clay, crushed granite, sand, and gravel, most of which is used in construction. Gemstones such as emeralds, rubies, and sapphires are also mined in the mountains.

Day-trippers visit some of Alexander County's mines and try to strike it rich.

Products & Resources

Tobacco

Even though North Carolina grows less tobacco each year, it is still the state's number one crop. North Carolina grows more tobacco than any other state.

Turkeys

Poultry is big business in the state. Farmers raise about 40 million turkeys a year. This makes North Carolina the nation's second-largest producer of this popular Thanksgiving bird.

Sweet Potatoes

The sweet potato is North Carolina's official vegetable. The tuber is also a valuable crop for the state. North Carolina produces about 45 percent of the nation's sweet potatoes, mostly in the coastal counties.

Textiles

Although the United States does not manufacture as much clothing and fabric as it once did, North Carolina is still a leading textile manufacturer. Hanesbrands operates from Winston-Salem, and Cotton Incorporated calls Cary its home. Cotton Incorporated is the nation's leading organization that researches cotton and promotes the use of products made from cotton.

Computers and Electronic Products

Businesses in North Carolina create billions of dollars' worth of computer hardware and software. Thousands of residents write computer operating systems and programs. Even more make computers and the microchips that power them.

Minerals

North Carolina mines produce large quantities of feldspar and crude mica, minerals that are sold around the world. Feldspar is used in making glass and ceramics, and mica is used in paint, plastics, and cement.

Banking

The first banks opened in North Carolina at New Bern and Wilmington in 1804. The state became an important center for banking in the 1950s and 1960s. Today, Charlotte, Greensboro, Raleigh, and Winston-Salem are all banking centers, with company headquarters that provide many high-paying jobs. Bank of America, the largest bank in the country, is headquartered at Charlotte.

Manufacturing

In the decades after the Civil War, North Carolina began shifting from a farming economy to manufacturing. Manufacturing cigarettes, fabric, and furniture were three important industries for much of the twentieth century.

Manufacturing is still important in the state. However, the focus has shifted to high-tech products and biotechnology. Many of these industries are located in the Research Triangle area, where Raleigh, Durham, and Chapel Hill are located. Students who attend the state's nine research universities and five medical schools also make valuable contributions in these fields.

Biotechnologists use living organisms such as plants and bacteria to make new medicines, vaccines, or even food. GlaxoSmithKline, one of the world's largest pharmaceutical companies, has a headquarters and research facility in Research Triangle Park. High-tech workers in the state develop new technologies and make cutting-edge electronic products. These include fiber optics, computer hardware and software, lasers, and robots.

Tourism and Entertainment

Tourists spend billions of dollars in North Carolina every year. Many visitors come to see the state's natural wonders and historic sites. Throughout the year, vacationers travel to North Carolina to enjoy the outdoors and the mild climate, from the beaches to the mountains. Sporting events also attract many visitors. History is recreated across the state in outdoor stage productions ranging from *The Lost Colony* on Roanoke Island to *Unto These Hills*, the story of the Cherokees. Nearly 200,000 people have jobs in the tourism industry.

The Charlotte financial district is home to the headquarters of Bank of America.

The popular CW Network television show *One Tree Hill* is filmed in Wilmington.

The state has also become a popular spot for filming movies and television shows. More than eight hundred movies and fifteen television series have been shot in North Carolina. In fact, the country's biggest studio outside California is in Wilmington.

"One North Carolina"

North Carolina is home to all sorts of people. Yet, whatever they do, however they choose to live, the people of North Carolina stand united in their great pride for their state. Residents value the ways in which they each differ but believe that, deep down, "We are one North Carolina."

State Flag & Seal

North Carolina's current state flag was designed in 1885 and changed slightly in 1991. The right-hand side of the flag has a horizontal red stripe with a white stripe below it. The left-hand side has a vertical blue stripe. In the center of the stripe is a white star with the letters N and C in gold. "May 20th 1775" is written above the letters and star. This is said to be the date when Mecklenburg County declared independence from Great Britain. "April 12th 1776" is written below the letters and star. This was the date that North Carolinians adopted the Halifax Resolves.

The state seal, which features two women, was designated in 1971. The woman on the left represents liberty. In one hand, she holds a pole with a red cap (two symbols of liberty). In the other, she holds a scroll with the word "Constitution" on it. The other woman represents plenty. She holds three stalks of grain and a cornucopia, a horn full of crops. Behind the women are mountains that descend to a ship on the ocean. The state motto appears along the bottom of the seal. It means "To be, rather than to seem." The dates on the state flag are also found on the seal.

NORTH CAROLINA

State Song

The Old North State

words and music by William Joseph Gaston

BOOKS

Cannavale, Matthew C. *North Carolina, 1524-1776*. Washington, D.C.: National Geographic Society, 2007.

Dixon-Engel, Tara; and Mike Jackson. *The Wright Brothers: First in Flight*. New York: Sterling, 2007.

Miller, Lee. *Roanoke: Mystery of the Lost Colony*. New York: Scholastic, 2007.

Stewart, Mark. *The North Carolina Tar Heels*. Chicago: Norwood House, 2010.

Zepke, Terrance. *Pirates of the Carolinas for Kids*. Sarasota, FL: Pineapple Press, 2009.

WEBSITES

LEARN NC, University of North Carolina at Chapel Hill School of Education:
http://www.learnnc.org

North Carolina Department of Cultural Resources:
http://www.ncdcr.gov

North Carolina Museum of History:
http://ncmuseumofhistory.org

State of North Carolina Official Website:
http://www.ncgov.com

The Way We Lived in North Carolina, North Carolina Office of Archives & History:
http://www.waywelivednc.com

Ann Graham Gaines is a freelance writer and picture researcher, whose first book for children was published in 1991. She and her family live in Texas. North Carolina is one of her favorite places to visit.

Andy Steinitz has written and edited educational and reference materials for *The World Almanac*, Borders Books, and the *New York Times*. He has visited North Carolina several times. He finds the view from Chimney Rock and the vinegar pulled pork equally inspiring. Steinitz currently works at Pratt Institute. He lives in Brooklyn, NY.

Page numbers in **boldface** are illustrations.